THE LITTLE GREEN BOOK

The astonishing beliefs of the man who has shaken the Western world.

Ayatollah Khomeini

THE LITTLE GREEN BOOK

Selected Fatawah
And Sayings of The

Ayatollah Mosavi Khomeini

— translated into English by Harold Salemson —
with a special introduction by Clive Irving

Bantam Books, 1985 / ISBN: 0553140329

PDF Edition by

KULTURAL FREEDOM

TABLE OF CONTENTS

INTRODUCTION

The Little Green Book is a collection of fatawah handed down by the most prominent and arguably one of the most influential Muslim clerics in modern history; the Grand Ayatollah Seyyed Ruhollah Mosavi Khomeini, commonly known as the Ayatollah Khomeini. *Fatawah* (the plural of *fatwah*) are Islamic religious decrees sent down by Muslim religious leaders. Since Islam demands that Muslims abide by *Sharia* – Islamic law as individuals and as a society, these fatawah are not simply religious insights or advice. They are legal pronouncements, and define the law of the land in an Islamic country. In his unrivaled role as Iran's Supreme Leader and the highest-ranking cleric for Shi'a Muslims, the Ayatollah Khomeini's *fatawah* guided the lives of more Shi'a Muslims than did any other Islamic leader throughout history.

It would have been damning to Islam if these inane, absurd, and depraved rantings had come from any Muslim, since they would serve as an example of how Islam corrupts a person's mind. Beyond that however, anyone who takes the time to analyze Islam's scriptures and what is recorded in Islam about Muhammad, the man whose life sets the standard to which Muslims are to strive, will see that the Ayatollah Khomeini was not off-base in his Islamic jurisprudence.

This version of *The Little Green Book*, is a translation done by Harold Salemson, whose source was a French translation of the Ayatollah's fatawah compiled by a Persian named Jean-Marie Xaviere. The book is broken up into two volumes. The first volume deals with governing issues, and is so chock full of amazing quotes, we had to give up on trying to highlight the best ones. The second volume focuses on lifestyle guidelines, and tends to be a bit mundane. However, some of the more astoundingly reprehensible whoppers are in this section. Additionally, the emphasis placed on defining even the most miniscule details for a Muslim to follow serve as a tremendous example of how Islam thrives on replacing every last iota of independent thought with mindless servitude. Of course, this should not come as a surprise to anyone, since the religion's name literally means "Submission" (Islam), and its followers refer to themselves as "those who *submit*" (Muslims).

The Little Green Book is a quick read. In fact, it's probably shorter than some of Craig Winn's email responses. Additionally, much of it is so absurd, it's quite entertaining. That is, until you realize that this isn't a joke and you remember that billions of people are affected by these fatawah and thousands more like them from multitudes of other Islamic leaders.

Clive Irving

I. 1
ISLAM AS A REVOLUTIONARY RELIGION

Islam is a religion of those who struggle for truth and justice, of those who clamor for liberty and independence. It is the school of those who fight against colonialism.

Our one and only remedy is to bring down these corrupt and corrupting systems of government, and to overthrow the traitorous, repressive, and despotic gangs in charge. This is the duty of Muslims in all Islamic countries; this is the way to victory for all Islamic revolutions.

Muslims have no alternative, if they wish to correct the political balance of society, and force those in power to conform to the laws and principles of Islam, to an armed Jihad against profane governments.

Though you may not have the means to prevent heresy or fight corruption, nevertheless, you must not remain silent. If they hit you in the head, protest! Resigning yourself to oppression is more immoral than oppression itself. Argue, denounce, oppose, shout. Spread the truth – that Islamic justice is not what they say it is.

Jihad means the conquest of all non-Muslim territories. Such a war may well be declared after the formation of an Islamic government worthy of that name, at the direction of the Imam or under his orders. It will then be the duty of every able-bodied adult male to volunteer for this war of conquest, the final aim of which is to put Qur'anic law in power from one end of the earth to the other. But the whole world should understand that the universal supremacy of Islam is considerably different from the hegemony of other conquerors. It is therefore necessary for the Islamic government first to be created under the authority of the Imam in order that he may undertake this conquest, which will be distinguishable from all other wars of conquest, which are unjust and tyrannical and disregard the moral and civilizing principles of Islam.

Who liberated our country and our people from the shame of Zoroastrianism, if not the victorious army of Islam?

There are some of us who aren't concerned with developing an Islamic movement, but, instead, of making the pilgrimage to Mecca with the Muslim brothers, in peace and understanding. It certainly wasn't that way in the time of the Prophet. The Friday prayers were the means of mobilizing the people, of inspiring them to battle. The man who goes to war straight from the mosque is afraid of only one thing – Allah. Dying, poverty, and homelessness mean nothing to him; an army of men like that is a victorious army.

Islamic faith and justice demand that within the Muslim world, anti-Islamic governments not be allowed to survive. The installation of a lay public power is equivalent to actively opposing the progress of Islamic order. Any nonreligious power, whatever form or shape it may take, is necessarily an atheistic power, the tool of Satan; it is part of our duty to stand in its path and to struggle against its effects. Such Satanic power can engender nothing but corruption on earth, the supreme evil which must be pitilessly fought and rooted out. To achieve that end, we have no recourse other than to overthrow all governments that do not rest on pure Islamic principles, and are thus traitorous, rotten, unjust, and tyrannical administrative systems that server them. That is not only our duty in Iran, but it is also the duty of all Muslims in the world, in all Muslim countries, to carry the Islamic political revolution to its final victory.

I. 2
ISLAM AND COLONIALISM

Europe [the West] is nothing but a collection of unjust dictatorships; all of humanity must strike these troublemakers with an iron hand if it wishes to regain its tranquility. If Islamic civilization had governed the West, we would no longer have to put up with these barbaric goings-on unworthy even of wild animals.

At a time in the West so primitive that there is no recorded history of it, when its inhabitants were still wild, and when America was still a land of half-wild redskins, the peoples of the Persian and Roman empires were forced to live under despotism, oligarchy, favoritism, and absolute rule, without the slightest participation or right to participate in their own government. It was then that Allah, through his prophet, sent us the laws whose scope has amazed mankind.

The homeland of Islam, one and indivisible, was broken up by the doings of the Imperialists and despotic and ambitious leaders. The Muslim people, one and indivisible, was broken up into several peoples. And when the Ottoman Empire struggled to achieve Islamic unity, it as opposed by a united front of Russian, English, Austrian, and other imperialist powers, which split it up among themselves.

Western missionaries, carrying out secret plans drawn up centuries ago, have created religious schools of their own within Muslim countries. We did not react against that, and this is what it led to: These missionaries infiltrated our villages and our countrysides, to turn our children into Christians or atheists!

The Islamic movement met its first saboteur in the Jewish people, who are at the source of all the anti-Islamic libels and intrigues current today. Then came the turn of those even more damnable representatives of Satan, the imperialists. Within the last three centuries or more, they have invaded every Muslim country, with the intention of destroying Islam. They have been aware ever since the Crusades that only Islam, with its laws and its faith, can bar the way to their material interests and political power. They sent missionaries into Muslim cities, and there found accomplices within the universities and various information or publication centers, mobilized their Orientalist scholars in the service of imperialism – all of that only so as to distort Islamic truths.

Their plan is to keep us in our backward state, to preserve our backward state, to preserve our pathetic way of life, so they can exploit the tremendous wealth of our underground resources, of our land, and our manpower. They want us to stay destitute, distracted by niggling day-to-day problems of survival, our poor living in misery, so that we will never become aware of the laws of Islam – which contain the solution to misery and poverty! All of this they have done so they can sit in their big palaces, living their stupid shallow lives!

Many of these corruptions have their origin in the gang that is in power, and in the family of a despotic and capricious ruler. These are the rulers who create hotbeds of lust, prostitution, and drugs, who devote the revenues of the mosque to building cinemas!

Islam does not have kings or crown princes. If that's a fault, well then, Islam is a faulty religion!

What do you understand of the harmony between social life and religious principles? And more important, just what is the social life we are talking about? Is it those hotbeds of immorality called theaters, cinemas, dancing, and music? Is it the promiscuous presence in the streets of lusting young men and women with arms, chests, and thighs bared? Is it the ludicrous wearing of a hat like the Europeans or the imitation of their habit of wine drinking? We are convinced that you have been made to lose your ability to distinguish between good and evil, in exchange for a few radio sets and ludicrous Western hats. Your attention has been attracted to the disrobed women to be seen on thoroughfares ad in swimming pools. Let these shameful practices come to an end, so that the dawn of a new life may break!

All governments of the world rely upon the power of their bayonets. We know of no monarchy or republic in the world today which is based upon equity and reason; and all maintain themselves in power only through oppression.

The leaders of our country have been so deeply influenced by the West that they have regulated the standard time of their country upon that of Europe (Greenwich Mean Time). What a nightmare!

In the past century, during which European medicine and surgery have been introduced into Iran, our leaders have forgotten our traditional medicine and encouraged a handful of inexperienced young men to study this cursed European medicine. Today we realize that illnesses such as typhus, typhoid fever, and the like are curable only by traditional remedies.

The clergy must undertake no functions other than religious ones which serve monotheism, virtue, the teaching of divine laws, and the uplifting of public morals. The army must also be under the control of the clergy in order to be efficacious and useful.

We [clergy] forcefully affirm that refusal to wear the veil is against the law of Allah and the Prophet, and a material and moral affront to the entire country. We affirm that the ludicrous use of the Western hat stands in the way of our independence and is contrary to the will of Allah. We affirm that coeducational schools are an obstacle to a wholesome life; they are a material and moral affront to the country and contrary to the divine will. We affirm that music engenders immorality, lust, and licentiousness, and stifles courage, valor, and the chivalrous spirit; it is forbidden by Qur'anic law and must not be taught in the schools. Radio Tehran, by broadcasting Western, Oriental, and Iranian music, plays a nefarious role by introducing immorality and licentiousness into respectable families.

Ulamas [scholars] and other ecclesiastics are not permitted to run the theology schools set up by the state. State intervention in this domain is always a pretext for the destruction of the foundations of

Islam on orders of the imperialists. This happens in all Muslim countries without exception.

Members of the clergy who, wearing clerical garb, cooperate in one way or another with such schools of theology must be shinned by all true Muslims. It is forbidden to associate with them, to indulge in collective prayer in their presence, to make use of their services for the repudiation of one's wife, to pay legal alms to them, to invite them to officiate at funeral ceremonies, or to listen to their sermons at meetings organized by the state with the sole intent of having them preach lies and diabolical anti-Islamic thoughts.

We see today that Jews – may Allah bring them down! – have manipulated the editions of the Qur'an published in their occupied zones. We have to protest, to make everyone understand that these Jews are bent upon the destruction of Islam and the establishment of a universal Jewish government. And since they are a cunning and active people, I fear – may Allah protect us from it! – that sooner or later they may succeed in attaining this goal, that through the weakness of some among us we may one day find ourselves under Jewish rule – Allah preserve us from it!

Some scholarly Orientalists, agents in the pay of the imperialists, are working to transform the Islamic truths. The missionaries, those other agents of imperialism, are also busy throughout the Muslim world in perverting our youth, not by converting them to their own religion, but by corrupting them. And that is the very thing imperialists are after. In Teheran itself, propaganda centers for Christianity, Zionism, and Bahaism, have been set up for the sole purpose of luring the faithful away from the commandments of Islam. Is it not our duty to destroy all these hotbeds of danger to Islam?

I. 3
THE ISLAMIC REPUBLIC

An Islamic government cannot be totalitarian or despotic, but is constitutional and democratic. In this democracy, however, the laws are not made by the will of the people, but only by the Qur'an and the Sunnah [Traditions] of the Prophet. The constitution, the civil code, and the criminal code should be inspired only by Islamic laws contained in the Qur'an and transcribed by the Prophet. Islamic government is the government of divine right, and its laws cannot be changed, modified, or contested.

In any self-respecting Islamic government, the legislative, executive, and judicial branches are replaced by a Religious Planning Council. The council keeps each cabinet department informed of the Islamic laws affecting it, indicates what its program must be in conformity with religious law, and on the basis of the totality of these programs establishes general policy for the whole country.

The Islamic government is subject to the law of Islam, which comes neither from the people nor from its representatives, but directly from Allah and His divine will. Qur'anic law, which is nothing other than divine law, constitutes the essence of any Islamic government and unfailingly governs all individuals who are a part of it. The Prophet, the Caliphs [spiritual heads of Islam], and the people all owe absolute obedience to these eternal laws of the Almighty, transmitted to mortals through the Qur'an and the Prophet, which remain immutable until the end of time.

It is often proclaimed that religion must be separated from politics, and that the ecclesiastical world should keep out of affairs of state. It is proclaimed that high Muslim clerical authorities have no business mixing into the social and political decisions of the government. Such proclamations can come only from atheists; they are dictated and spread by imperialists. Was politics separate from religion in the time of the Prophet (God salute him, him and his faithful)? Was there a distinction at that time between the religious and the high functionaries of the state? Were religious and temporal powers separate in the times of the Caliphs? Those are aberrations invented by the imperialists with a view to turning the clergy away from the material and social life of Muslim peoples, and thus to getting a free hand to pillage their wealth.

Think of it – a political clergy! Well, why not? The Prophet was a politician!

He (The Prophet) appointed governors to provinces, formed tribunals and named judges, set up embassies in other countries, and sent ambassadors to other tribes and kings... In short, all the normal functions of government.

In order to ensure the unity of the Muslim people, to liberate the Islamic homeland from the domination of the influence of imperialists, we have no other way out than to form a true Islamic government, do whatever is necessary to overthrow the other tyrannical pseudo-Muslim governments put in place by foreigners, and once this goal is attained to install the universal Islamic government.

We have nothing against going to the moon, or setting up atomic installations. But we too have a mission to accomplish: the mission of serving Islam and making its sacred principles known to the entire world, in the hope that all the monarchs and presidents of republics throughout the Muslim world will finally recognize that our cause is just, and by that very fact become submissive to us. Naturally, we have no desire to strip them of their functions; we will allow them to retain power, provided they show themselves to be obedient and worthy of our confidence.

It the enemy attacks the borders of an Islamic country, it is the sacred duty of all Muslims in the world to defend it by every means in their power, by giving of their wealth or of their persons. They need await no permission to fulfill this duty.

If within a Muslim country, diabolical foreign plans are fomented, and if there is any fear that these may lead to foreign domination, it is the duty of every Muslim to work against such plans.

If as a result of the political, economic, or commercial influence of foreigners, there is the risk of seeing the latter gain control over the destinies of Islamic countries, it is the duty of every Muslim to defend the interests at stake and bar the path to any foreign intrusion.

If there is a justified fear that the diplomatic relations of Muslim states with foreign states might lead to the predominance of the latter within Muslim countries, even if such predominance be only political or economic, all Muslims must oppose such a situation with force, and compel the Islamic governments to sever such diplomatic relations.

If there comes to be a justified concern that commercial relations with foreigners might be harmful to Islamic markets and lead to commercial or economic dependence, such relations must be broken off and such commerce proclaimed to be religiously illicit.

If establishing political or commercial relations between a Muslim and a non-Muslim country is not in the interests of Islam and Muslims, such relations are forbidden; if a country allows them, it is the duty of all other Muslim countries to force it by ever means within their power to sever such relations.

If certain chiefs of state of Muslim countries or certain members of parliament favor a foreign political, economic, or military influence, which is inevitably against the interests of Islam and of all Muslims, they must for such treason be removed from their functions, whatever these may be, even though they may have acceded to them through entirely legal means. It is the duty of all Muslims to punish such individuals by ever possible means.

It is forbidden for any Muslim state to have commercial and diplomatic relations with countries which play the role of puppets for the great powers – as is the case with Israel – and it is the duty of all Muslims to oppose such relations by every means available; any businessman having commercial dealing with Israel, its representatives, or its agents is a traitor to Islam and to all other Muslims, because he is contributing to the destruction of Islam. It is the duty of all Muslims to sever their relations with such traitors, whether they be states or businessmen, with a view to forcing them to repent.

All the laws approved and passed until now by the two chambers of the Iranian Parliament, on the orders of foreign agents – Allah punish them! – contrary to the texts of the Qur'an and the law of the Holy Prophet of Islam are hereby proclaimed null and void from the Islamic viewpoint. It is the duty of all the faithful to turn against all those who supported them, to isolate such people, not to rub elbows with them or have any business dealings with them, and to consider them as malefactors. Even going near them is in itself a cardinal sin.

I. 4
THE RULE OF THE CLERGY

If religious experts of wisdom and justice devoted themselves to the Islamic law and to setting up an Islamic law and to setting up an Islamic state, never again would the people go hungry.

It is written that "the clergy rule the sultans." If the sultans are obedient to Islam, then they should also be obedient to the clergy; they should ask the clergy for laws and regulations and advice on how to apply them. In this way he clergy are the real leaders and power belong to them, officially.

You (the clergy) have the duty to establish an Islamic state. Have confidence in yourselves: you are perfectly capable of assuming that burden. We will do as the colonialists did three or four hundred years ago – they started from nothing and got to this point. We too will start from nothing. Don't let yourselves be intimidated by a handful of your fellow countrymen who have sold out to the West, who are the valets of imperialism. Explain to the people that the clergy are not going to sit in a corner at Qom or An Najaf studying unimportant matters like the rules governing the menstruation of omen, and cutting themselves off from politics because "religion and politics should be separate."

Are those who govern in Muslim countries these days any more capable than we are? Who among them has more aptitude than the average man? Many of them never even went to school... Mr. Reza [Rezah Shah – the Shah's father] was nothing but an uneducated buck private. Historically this has often been the case. Many despots and absolute rulers had neither the aptitude to run a country, nor common sense, nor knowledge nor wisdom. Harun al-Rashid [A renowned 19th century Caliph in Baghdad] or others like him, what did they go through in the way of an education? TO administer laws and govern a country, you need a solid educational grounding.

In certain cases deception is necessary for the maintenance of Islam and of religion in general; without it faith could not survive.

If anyone, in the guise of pursuing Islamic justice, interprets the Law in a manner contrary to the divine will, he has committed the sin of innovation. Learned men are bound to condemn him or they will themselves be condemned.

Given that the clergy occupy a lower position (than the Prophet of the Imam), should they therefore punish an offense less severely? Can we say that the Prophet ought to order a hundred and fifty lashes, Ali a hundred lashes, and the clergy only fifty, in a case when the penalty should be one hundred lashes? No. The chief magistrate possesses executive power that is always in accordance with divine standards, whether he be the Prophet, Ali, or the duly constituted representative.

I. 5
The Imam

We need a head of government who is not at the mercy of his lust and other temptations. We need someone to govern us for whom all are equal, for whom all enjoy the same rights and obligations; someone who doesn't indulge in favoritism, who regards his family in the same light as others, who will cut off his son's hands if he steals, and execute his brothers and sisters if they sell heroin.

As far as function and rank are concerned, there is no difference between the guardian of a minor and the guardian of an entire people. Leading the government or indeed occupying any official position is like the Imam and his appointees taking care of children.

The great scholars, those "fortresses of Islam," are the embodiment of Islamic faith as well as its guardians They affirm Islamic principles in their emotional and moving sermons and through the special nature of their leadership. That's why, when after a long life, perhaps even more than a hundred years, they die, that death is a great blow to Islam, and why the faithful experience an immense lack in their absence. But if it's a question of my death, I who do nothing but sit in a corner of my house studying; what lack will the faithful fell in my absence?

The Imams were shining lights in the darkness of the heavens, infinitely gifted and by birth and nature superior to other men – much so that even the angel Gabriel declared "If I came too close to them, I would be burned."

The leaders of the USSR and of England and the president of the United States are invested with power (like the Imam), but they are infidels. They wield their political power and influence in order to fulfill sordid personal ambitions, which they accomplish by administering inhuman laws and using inhuman political methods. But the Imam and the clergy have the duty to use the political apparatus to apply the laws of Allah and to bring about a system of equality for the benefit of the people. Governing means nothing for them except pain and difficulty, but what can they do? The rule of the clergy is an obligation they must fulfill.

Since the Almighty did not designate anyone by name to form the Islamic government in the absence of the hidden Imam [the Twelfth Imam], what are we to do? But while Allah did not name anyone, He intended that the virtues characteristic of Islamic governments from the dawn of Islam to the reign of the Twelfth Imam be perpetrated. These virutes, these qualities, represented by perfect knowledge of law and justice, are to be found in many of the religious learned of our time. If those learned come together, they will be able to establish the authority that will bring about universal justice. If a competent man, combining in himself these supreme virtues, appears and founds a true Islamic government, it means that he has been invested as the Holy Prophet to lead the people; therefore, it is the people's absolute duty to follow him.

I. 6
ISLAMIC JUSTICE

In an Islamic government, all people are under the protection of the law. No one may endanger their safety, break into their houses, arrest them, imprison or exile them, or summarily execute them on the basis of a simple accusation or suspicion. Under such a government, everyone can have full confidence in the law of the Prophet, and no judge or dignitary dare act contrary to it.

The person who governs the Muslim community must always have its interests at heart and not his own. This is why Islam has put so many people to death: to safeguard the interests of the Muslim community. Islam has obliterated many tribes because they were sources of corruption and harmful to the welfare of Muslims.

Muslims are forbidden to seek redress of their grievances from the executive or judiciary of improperly constituted governments. They are forbidden to have legal recourse to kings or other despotic administrations, or to the judges that are appointed by them, even if they have legal rights to defend. A person whose son has been killed or whose house has been burgled may not seek justice from such courts, even if he is in the right and has conclusive evidence.

Islam has precepts for everything that concerns man and society. These come from the Almighty and are transmitted to men by His Prophet and Messenger. One may well be surprised by the majesty of these commandments, which cover every aspect of life, from conception to internment! There is no subject upon which Islam has not expressed judgment.

The Islamic republic is a government according to the Law and the wise men and theological experts of the clergy are therefore responsible for it. It is they who must watch over all aspects of administration and planning. In administering the laws of God in such matters as taxes and property for example, they must be trusted. Accordingly they must not allow delay in the execution of the Islamic laws, nor must thy be over lenient or over severe. If a member of the clergy wishes to inflict a penalty on someone, he must do so publicly, according to established practice, and lash him the specific number of times, without insulting him or slapping him or imprisoning him even for a single day.

Islamic justice is based on simplicity and ease. It settles all criminal or civil complaints in the most convenient, elementary, and expeditious way possible. All that is required is for an Islamic judge, with a pen and inkwell and two or three enforcers, to go into a town, come to his verdict on any kind of case, and have it immediately carried out. Look at the present cost in time and money in Western society with all its judicial procedures surrounding any judgment, in the name of principles alien to Islam!

If the punitive laws of Islam were applied for only one year, all the devastating injustices and immoralities would be uprooted. Misdeeds must be punished by the law of retaliation: cut off the hands of the thief; kill the murderer instead of putting him in prison; flog the adulterous woman or man. Your concerns, your "humanitarian" scruples are more childish than reasonable. Under the terms of Qur'anic law, any judge fulfilling the seven requirements (that he have reached puberty, be a believer, know the Qur'anic laws perfectly, be just, and not be affected by amnesia, or be a bastard, or be of the female sex) is qualified to dispense justice in any type of case. He can thus judge and dispose of twenty trials in a single day, whereas Occidental justice might take years to argue them out.

Ali [son-in-law of Muhammad], having cut off the hands of two thieves, treated their wounds and offered them his hospitality, and this affected them so much that they became utterly devoted to him; or again when he heard the marauding army of Muawiyah had abused a woman of one of the tribes, he was so upset and moved to pity that he declared: "If a man died after such an occurrence, no one cold blame him." And yet, despite a nature as sensitive as that, Ali bared his sword and hacked the perpetrators to pieces. This is the meaning of justice.

I. 7
YOUTH

Students have got their eyes open. If you present them with [the case for an Islamic republic], they will embrace it eagerly. Our students are against despotism, against repressive and colonialist authorities, against the ruffians who pillage the property of the people, against the Hars who consume impurities. There is no student or university that opposes an Islam founded on teachings such as ours and run according to social principles such as ours.

Our young people have the duty to rip the turban from the heads of those who, by pretending to be holy men and religious experts of Islam, are causing so much corruption among Muslims. I don't know if our youth is still alive! In my day it was never thus. Why don't they rip off those turbans? I don't say we should kill them, they are not worth killing. But our brave youth must see to it that such mullahs do not appear in public wearing the turban. It's not necessary to hit them too much, but those turbans must come off!

Put aside your sadness and resignation! Improve your programs and methods of spreading Islam! Make greater efforts to give it a fair presentation! Do your part: be the front-runners in setting up an Islamic republic. Put your hands in the hands of fighting and independent peoples!

Young boys or girls in full sexual effervescence are kept from getting married before they reach legal age of majority. This is against the intention of divine laws. Why should the marriage of pubescent girls and boys forbidden because they are still minors, when they are allowed to listen to the radio and to sexually arousing music?

You, young people of the new generation, try to think more clearly. Stop turning toward science and its laws which have led so many among you to neglect your major responsibilities! Come to the help of Islam! Save the Muslims! The missionaries of different denominations, who are in service of the imperialists just as their local agents are, have spread to the four corners of the country.to turn our youth away from the path of righteousness and keep them from the service of Islam. Save that youth!

I. 8
MEDIA AND PROPAGANDA

We have a duty to create an Islamic republic and to that end our first obligation is the creation of a system of propaganda. This has always been the way things work. Once a few people sit down together, think matters out together, make decisions, it follows that propaganda will emerge. Then little by little others who think the same way are attracted to the group and it increases in size. Ultimately the group and its propaganda becomes a force that can infiltrate a huge system of government or even bring about its downfall.

Radio and television are allowed if they are used for the broadcasting of news or sermons, for the spreading of good educational material for publicizing the products and curiosities of the planet; but they must prohibit singing, music, anti-Islamic laws, the lauding of tyrants, mendacious words, and broadcasts which spread doubt and undermine virtue.

Since the use of radio and television sets is not carried out in conformity with the above-mentioned principles, the trade in them is limited to those who will put them to good use and who will see to it that others follow in the same path.

II. 9
On Urinating and Defecating

It is required that everyone, when urinating or defecating, hide his sexual parts from all pubescent persons, even his sister or his mother, as well as from any feebleminded person or children too young to understand. But husband and wife are not required to hide from each other.

It is not indispensable to hide one's genitals with anything in particular; one's hand is enough.

When defecating or urinating, one must squat in such a way as neither to face Mecca nor turn one's back upon it.

It is not sufficient to turn one's sex organ away, while oneself facing or turning one's back on Mecca; and one's privates must never be exposed either facing Mecca or facing directly away from Mecca.

Urinating and defecating are forbidden in four places: blind alleys, except with the permission of those living along them; the property of a person who has not given permission to do so; places of worship, such as a certain *medersas* [Arabic schools]; graves of believers, unless one does so as an insult to them.

In three cases, it is absolutely necessary to purify one's anus with water: when the excrement has been expelled with other impurities, such as blood, for example; when some impure thing has grazed the anus; when the anal opening has been soiled more than usual.

Apart from these three cases, one may either was one's anus with water or wipe it with some fabric or a stone.

The urinary orifice can be cleaned off only with water, and it is enough to wash it just one time after urinating. But those in whom the urine comes out through some other orifice would do better to wash that orifice at least twice. This must be observed by women as well.

It is not necessary to wipe one's anus with three stones or with three pieces of fabric: a single stone or single piece of fabric is enough. But if one wipes with a bone, or any sacred object, such as, for example, a paper having the name of Allah on it, one may not say his prayers while in this state.

It is preferable, for urinating or defecating, to squat down in an isolated place; it is also preferable to go into this place with the left foot first, and come out of it with the right foot first; it is recommended that one keep his head covered while evacuating, and have the weight of his body carried by the left foot.

During evacuation, one must not squat facing the sun or the moon, unless one's genitals are covered. While defecating, one must also avoid squatting exposed to the wind, or in public places, or at the door one's house, or under a fruit tree. At the time of the evacuation, one must also avoid eating, dallying, or washing one's anus with the right hand. Finally, one must avoid talking, unless one is absolutely forced to or is addressing a prayer to Allah.

It is better to avoid urinating standing up or urinating into hard ground, or into an animal hole, or into ware, especially stagnant water.

It is recommended not to hold back the need to urinate or defecate, especially if it hurts.

It is recommended to urinate before prayers, before going to bed, before having sexual intercourse, and after ejaculating.

After urination, one must first wash the anus if it has been soiled by urine; then one must press three times with the middle finger of his left hand on the part between the anus and the base of the penis; then one must put his thumb on top of the penis and his index finger on the bottom and pull the skin forward three times as far as the circumcision ring; and after that three times squeeze the tip of the penis.

A woman has no special instructions to follow after urinating; if she afterward notes some moisture at the vaginal orifice which she cannot judge as pure or impure, the said moisture remains pure and in no way stands in the way of her performing ablutions or praying.

II. 10
On Eating and Drinking

There are eighteen principles to be observed at mealtime; washing one's hands before the meal; washing and drying one's hands after the meal; the head of the house beginning eating before any of his guests and finishing after them; he must wash his hands before the meal ahead of the others, and be followed by the person who sits at his right, and then the next, and so on, until reaching the one seated at his left; beginning the meal by invoking the name of Allah; but if several courses are served, it is recommended that this be repeated before each course; taking with one's right hand; eating with three fingers, leaving the other two free; taking small quantities of food in each mouthful; stretching the meal out as long as possible; chewing one's food at length; praising Allah at the end of the meal; licking one's fingers; cleaning one's teeth after the meal with a toothpick, which must not be made of pomegranate wood, basil wood, reed, or palm leaves; gathering up the remains of the meal in order to eat them later, but if the meal is eaten in the desert it is better to leave such remains for the birds and animals; eating at the beginning of the day and at nightfall, and abstaining therefrom during the day and during the night; resting on one's back after eating, and putting the right leg over the left; taking salt at the beginning and the end of the meal; washing all fruit before it.

There are eleven things to be avoided during meals; eating when one is not hungry; eating too much, which is frowned upon by the Almighty; watching others while eating; eating things that are too hot; blowing on a dish or into a glass to cool the food or drink; starting to eat as soon as the the bread has been put on the table; cutting bread with a knife; putting bread under one's plate; cleaning a meat bone so there is nothing left on it; peeling fruit; throwing away half-eaten fruit.

There are six principles to be observed while drinking water: sucking it up rather than gulping it down; drinking upright invoking the name of Allah before and after drinking; drinking in three steps; drinking of one's own free will; recalling the martyrdom of Hazrat Abu Abdullah and his family, and cursing their murderers, after drinking.

There are five things to be avoided during the absorption of water: drinking to excess; drinking after a heavy meal; drinking standing up during the night; taking the water jug in one's left hand; drinking from a place where the jug is chipped or broken or at the location of the handle.

Among the organs of fowl, game, domestic animals, fish, and so on whose flesh of you are permitted to eat, there are fifteen which are proscribed: blood; excrement; the penis; the vagina; the uterus; the glands; the testicles; the central part of the brain; the little chickpea-shaped ball at the back side of the brain; the nerves located on either side of the spinal column; the gallbladder; the liver; the bladder; the eye; matter accumulated under the claws.

It is forbidden to consume the excrement of animals or their nasal secretions. But if such are mixed in minute proportions into other foods their consumption is not forbidden.

The meat of horses, mules, or donkeys is not recommended. It is strictly forbidden if the animal was sodomized while alive by a man. In that case, the animal must be taken outside the city and sold.

If one commits an act of sodomy with a cow, a ewe, or a camel, their urine and their excrements become impure, and even their milk may no longer be consumed. The animal must then be killed as quickly as possible and burned, and the price of it paid to its owner by him who sodomized it.

Drinking wine or alcoholic beverages is a mortal sin, and is strictly forbidden. Whoever consumes an alcoholic beverage retains only a part of his soul, that part of it which is deformed and nasty; he is damned by Allah, His archangels, His prophets, and His believers. Such a man's daily prayers are rejected by Allah for forty days. On the day of the resurrection of the dead, his face will turn black, his tongue will hang out of his mouth, his saliva will run down his chest, and he will remain forever thirsty.

II. 11
On Pure and Impure Things

There are eleven things which are impure: urine, excrement, sperm, bones, blood, dogs, pigs, non-Muslim men and women, wine, beer, and the sweat of the excrement-eating camel.

The urine and feces of man and any animal whose blood spurts when a vein or artery of its body is opened are impure. But flyspecks or the droppings of mosquitoes or other such small insects whose blood does not gush are pure.

The urine and feces of any excrement-eating animal are impure. This is equally true of the urine and feces of any animal which has been sexually possessed by a human; and of the urine and feces of sheep which have been fed on sow's milk.

The sperm of any animal whose blood spurts when its throat is cut is impure.

The bones of an animal found dead or an animal slaughtered otherwise than according to Muslim rites are impure; fish, on the other hand, is never impure, even if found dead in the water, for its blood does not spurt.

The hairs, bones, and teeth of dead animals are pure, unless they come from animals such as the dog which are impure themselves.

The egg taken from the entrails of a chicken is not impure, provided its shell is sufficiently hard. However, it must be washed before being eaten.

The meat, fat, and skins on sale in a Muslim bazaar on being handled by a Muslim are pure, unless such products come from animals which were not slaughtered according to the Muslim rites.

The blood of man and any animal whose blood spurts when the throat is cut is impure; on the other hand, the blood of the fish, mosquito, or any other animal whose blood does not spurt remains pure.

The blood that may flow out between one's teeth is pure if diluted with saliva; it is permitted to swallow that saliva.

Blood coagulated and accumulated under the nails or in any other part of the human body is pure if its appearance has been so modified that one can no longer call it blood; if that is not the case, every effort must be made to rid oneself of it before performing one's ablutions.

The pus of a healing wound is pure, provided one can be sure it is not mixed with blood.

Dog and pig, unless they live in water, are impure, as are their hairs, their bones, their claws, and their excrements; on the other hand, sea dogs and pigs are pure.

Every part of the body of a non-Muslim individual is impure, even the hair on his hand and his body hair, his nails, and all the secretions of the body.

Any man or woman who denies the existence of Allah, or believes in His partners [the Christian Trinity], or else does not believe in His Prophet Muhammad, is impure (in the same way as are excrement, urine, dog, and wine). He is so even if he doubts any one of these principles.

A child who has not reached puberty is impure if his parents and grandparents are not Muslims, but if he has one Muslim in his ancestry he is pure.

A Muslim who insults one of the Twelve Imams or declares himself their enemy is impure.

Wine and all other intoxicating beverages are impure, but opium and hashish are not.

Beer is impure, but brewer's yeast is not.

The sweat of an excrement-eating animal is impure; the sweat of other animals, which do not eat the same detritus, is not.

The sweat of a man who has just ejaculated is not impure; yet it is preferable for him not to pray so long as his body or his clothing retain traces of that sweat.

If a man has had sexual relations with his wife during periods of prescribed abstinence, such as the fast of Ramadan, he must avoid saying his prayers so long as he still has upon him the traces of post-coital sweat.

If a part of the body that is sweating comes into contact with something impure and the sweat runs onto other parts of the body, all such parts become impure, although the rest of the body remains pure.

Bloodstained nasal secretions or expectorations are impure, whereas those which have not been soiled by blood are pure; if the nasal secretions or the expectoration touch the nose or mouth even lightly the part of the skin which has been so touch must be purified; but the untouched part remains pure.

An object which enters a human body and comes into contact with something impure (stool or blood) remains pure when withdrawn from that body if it has no traces of the impure matter left upon it; thus, the instrument introduced into the rectum for an enema or the surgeon's scalpel are not impure if they bear no trace of these impurities. The same applies to saliva or nasal secretions which mix with blood inside the mouth or nose, but show no trace of it when they are expectorated.

It is forbidden to touch a page of the Qur'an with anything impure; if such a thing should happen, the page must immediately be washed.

It is forbidden to place upon the Qur'an such impure matter as blood or human or animal bones if the matter is dried; should the matter already have been placed on it, it must absolutely be removed.

It is forbidden to write out verses of the Qur'an with impure ink, even though one write but one letter thereof. In case it has already been done, it must be washed away or erased with a knife or some other sharp instrument.

One must avoid giving the Qur'an to an infidel; it is even recommended that it be forcibly taken away from him if he already has it in his hands.

If a page of the Qur'an, or a piece of paper with the name of Allah or the Prophet or one of the Imams on it should fall into a toilet, it is absolutely indispensable to withdraw it from there, even if this should prove costly. In case this is impossible, such a toilet must never be used until it has been ascertained that the paper has rotted away.

It is forbidden to eat or drink anything that is impure; it is also forbidden to give anything impure to children to eat, whether or not it ay be harmful to them; but it is not forbidden to feed children food which has been only indirectly touched by something impure.

It is not required that one point out to a person that he is eating impure food or that he is praying while wearing impure clothing.

If the head of a household notices during the course of a meal that one or more of the dishes being served are impure, he must impart this information to his guests; but if it is one of the guest who notices it, he is not obliged to do the same.

II. 12
PURIFICATION

There are eleven elements or procedures which are purifying, that is, which erase impurities and make bodies and objects pure again: water; earth; sun; transmutation; reduction of grape juice by two-thirds' transfer; Islam; dependence; elimination of the impure object; keeping an animal from doing so for a specific period of time; absence of the Muslim.

Here are explanations of each element:

Water is purifying if it fulfills the following four conditions; it is pure (thus are watermelon juice and rose water not purifying); it is clean; after having been used to wash something impure, it has not been taken on the odor, color, or taste of that impure thing; after such washing, the remains of excrement or other detritus have left no traces in it.

An impure dish or container must be washed three times to regain its purity; but a container which has been licked by a dog or been used to give a dog his food or drink in, before being twice washed in water, must be rubbed first with earth. If a pig has used it, the dish must be washed seven times in succession but it need not be rubbed with earth. A container or glass which has held wine, and therefore is impure, must be washed three times, but it is better to wash it seven times. An oven which has become impure for having been urinate in regains its purity after twice being filled with water enough to cover all its sides. But if it has become impure from the contact of some other matter, such as excrement, it is enough to fill it with water once, after having removed the impure matter. If a thing becomes impure through having been soiled by the urine of a milk-fed boy (less than two years old), who has not drunk sow's milk, it is enough to wash it all over one time to purify it. Yet it is wise to wash it again a second time.

If the surface of a grain of wheat or rice or a piece of soap is soiled by some impurity, it is enough to plunge it into the amount of water required for purification in order for it to be pure again, but if the impurity has penetrated beneath its surface, this measure is not enough. If one cannot be absolutely sure that the impurity has penetrated deeply into the soap, the latter remains pure. Any impure object becomes pure only when the impure matter has been completely eliminated from it, but if the odor or color of the impure matter remains that makes no difference. The bits of impure food that remains between one's teeth after eating the food become pure if one washes his mouth with water so that all the impure remains are washed away.

If lump sugar has been made from impure melted sugar, the lump sugar remains impure even if placed in stagnant or running water.

Earth purifies the sole of the foot or shoe soiled with impurity, if it fulfills the following three conditions: it is pure; it is dry; and there is enough of it to eliminate the impure element (blood, urine, excrement, and such) from the sole of the foot or shoe. The earth may be muddy, firm, sandy, or pebbly; it is not enough to walk on a rug, or carpet, or grass, to purify the foot or shoe, as it is also not enough to walk on asphalt or flooring.

To purify the sole of the foot or shoe soiled by an impurity, one must take at least fifteen steps, even if the impurity disappears before fifteen steps.

For those who walk on their hands or knees, taking fifteen steps is not enough to purify their palms or their knees soiled by an impurity. The same applies to canes, crutches, horseshoes, wagon wheels, and so on. If after taking the fifteen steps, small bits of excrement or other detritus remain, they must be carefully removed, but the persistence of their odor or color makes no difference. The inside of the shoe, or the part of the sole of the foot which does not touch the ground, will not be purified by walking, and this also applies to socks, unless the part of the sock covering the sole of the foot is made of leather or hide.

Sun has purifying action on impure elements such as the ground, a building, doors, windows, nails stuck into walls, if the following six conditions are fulfilled: that the impure object be moist (if it is dry, it must be moistened so the sun may dry it); that the impurity is removed before the object is exposed to the rays of the sun; that these rays are not filtered through a curtain or through clouds, for example, unless it be an extremely thin cloud; that the impure object is dried exclusively by the rays of the sun, and not by the combined effort of sun and wind; that the sun dries all f the impure part of a building at one time (the façade may not be purified first, and the other walls only later); and, finally, that there is no intermediate element, such as air, within the thickness of the wall. If the sun has dried out impure ground, but later there is reason to question whether at the time it was moist or dry, or whether its moisture disappeared exclusively through the action of the rays of the sun or because of other factors, that ground remains impure; the same applies to ground or a building about which one cannot be sure that the impurities were removed from it before it was exposed to the sun, or whether the rays of the sun were able to play upon it directly. If only one of the walls was exposed to the sun, the other remains impure, unless the wall is so thin that drying one also dries the other.

Transmutation is a reaction by virtue of which an impure element is so completely transformed that it becomes something pure. This is the case of impure wood which in burning becomes transformed into pure ash, or of a dog which after being buried in saline ground turns into salt; but it does not apply to impure wheat which is made into flour or bread. Wine which turns to vinegar, whether on its own or due to the addition of salt or vinegar, is pure, but vinegar resulting from wine made of grapes soiled by urine or excrement, or from wine which has been mixed with such impurities, remains impure. Vinegar made with impure grapes, raisins, or dates remains impure. There is no objection to straw or small bits of the raisins being transformed into vinegar; nor is there any objection to cucumbers or eggplants being added to the dates, raisins, or grapes before they are made into vinegar.

Reduction of grape juice by two-thirds is purifying. Boiled grape juice is not impure even before having been reduced by two-thirds, but its consumption is forbidden if it is proven that it is intoxicating, in which case the juice can be purified only when it is turned into vinegar. The juice of an unripe bunch of grapes, even if the bunch has one or two ripe grapes on it, may be consumed, on condition that it first be boiled and that the sweet taste of the grape has disappeared.

Transfer is the operation by which the blood of a human being or any other animal the blood of which spurts when its throat is cut becomes pure by being transferred into the body of an insect the blood of which does not gush and becoming absorbed into the blood of the latter. On the other hand, human blood sucked by a leech remains impure even after its transfer into the body of the leech because it does not become absorbed into the blood of the leech.

If a person crushes a mosquito on his skin and cannot determine whether the blood therefrom is the insect's or his own, this blood is pure; but if the time between the bite and the death of the mosquito is so short that no such distinction can be made, the blood is impure.

Islam. A non-Muslim man or woman who becomes a convert to Islam automatically has a pure body, and pure saliva, nasal secretions, and perspiration. As for cohort's clothing, if it has been in contact with their sweating bodies before they became converted, it remains impure.

Dependence means the purification of one impure object being subject to the purification of another impure object. In the case of wine being turned into vinegar, the container having held the wine becomes pure once more up to the level reached by the wine turned vinegar. Thus, the piece of wood or stone on which mortuary ablutions are made, the fabric covering the genitals of the deceased, the hand of the person who has performed these ablutions, and the soap with which the corpse was washed, all become pure upon completion of the ritual.

The body of an animal or insect which was directly in contact with some impurity such as blood, or indirectly with impure water, becomes impure again as soon as the impure element is eliminated. The same holds true for the inside of a human mouth or nose. This means that if some blood runs out between one's teeth and dissolves in saliva, it is not necessary to wash one's mouth; if artificial teeth have been soiled by some impure matter, they must be taken out and washed. If bits of food remain between one's teeth and the inside of one's mouth bleeds, these bits of food are pure so long as one cannot be certain that the blood has touched them.

Keeping an animal which normally eats the excrement from doing so for a specific period of time. The urine and feces of such an animal are impure; in order for them to become pure, such animals must be kept from eating human excrement for forty days for a camel, twenty days for cattle, ten days for sheep, seven or five days for a turkey, and three days for a chicken.

Absence of the Muslim. If the clothing, kitchen utensils, or rugs belonging to a Muslim have been soiled by impure matter, and their owner is absent, they may not automatically be considered to be impure so long as one is not sure that they were not washed and purified before he left, or that they did not happen to fall into running water which purified them.

If one is certain that an object soiled by some impure matter has been purified, or if two trustworthy witnesses confirm that it has, the object becomes pure once again. This is also true of an impure object about which its owner asserts that it has been purified or that a Muslim has washed it, even if it cannot be established that he did so according to ritual.

One must not eat or drink out of any container made of pigskin or dog's hide, or any container made from the bone of any animal.

The remains of the food of dogs, pigs, and non-Muslim men and women are impure; the remains of the food of animals the flesh of which may be eaten are not impure, but it is nevertheless better to abstain therefrom.

II. 13
On the Nature of Water

There are two kinds of water; pure water, and water that is "in solution," such as, for instance, watermelon juice or attar of roses, or muddy water. Pure water is divided into five categories; stagnant water large enough in sufficient quantity; running water; rainwater; and well water.

Kor, or purifying water, is the quantity of water held in a container the length, width and depth of which each are 3½ *vadjabs* [about 70 centimeters or 27 inches]. This quantity of water should weigh about 128 maunds less 20 miskals [about 390 kilograms or 858 pounds].

If the above-mentioned water changes in taste, odor, or color because of impure contacts, such as with blood or urine, it becomes impure; but if it indirectly changes in odor, color, or taste because of some impure matter, for example if its odor is changed because of the proximity of some decomposing matter, it remains pure.

Water which has been polluted by blood, urine, or other impurities, and has thereby been changed in odor, color, or taste, is purified by running water or by rainwater which falls directly into it, or rainwater driven into it by the wind, or carried to it by a drainpipe, and thereby regains its purifying properties.

That a quantity of water is enough to be purifying may be established in one of two ways: either through one's own personal conviction that it is, or by two trustworthy men affirming that it is.

The water used for washing the urinary orifice and the anus remains pure in the five cases: if it has neither the odor, the color, nor the taste of urine or feces; if no external impurity has touched it; if no other impure matter such as blood issued from the anus or the urinary orifice at the same time as the excrement or urine; if no particles of excrement or urine are visible in the water; if the excrement that touched the anus as not exceptionally abundant.

Running water, even though in lesser quantity than that of purifying water, remains pure and therefore drinkable if it contains excrement or urine, provided however that the admixture of these has not altered its odor, color, or taste.

If excrement, urine, or other impurities have polluted running water, only that part of it which has been changed in odor, color, or taste becomes impure; the rest remains pure.

If excrement, urine, or any other impurity should be on the roof of a house and be rained upon, the rainwater remains pure if it continues falling and running directly off the roof or down a gutter or drainpipe; but if the rain stops, the water that continues running off and which is known to have touched the impurities on the roof is impure.

II. 14
On Ablution

[Body Purification]

There are two kinds of ablutions; the kind known as "step by step," which consists of washing the different parts of the body one after the other, and the kind known as "total," in which the whole body is immersed in water.

In step-by-step ablutions, one must begin by proclaiming in both loud and a low voice that one is planning to perform his ablutions; after that, one should wash one's head and the back of the neck, then the right side of the body, followed by the left side. If this precise order is not followed, whether deliberately or out of ignorance, the ablutions are not valid. It is to be pointed out that the right side of the navel and the right side of the genitals must be washed with the right side of the body, and the left side of the navel and genitals with the left side of the body. However, it is more prudent to was navel and genitals in their entirety along with each side of the body. If once the ablution is completed, one suspects that some part of the body has been overlooked, the ritual must be repeated; in that case, if the overlooked part is on the left side of the body, it is enough to wash only that part, but if it is on the right side of the body, after washing that part, the whole left side of the body must be washed again.

In a total ablution, one must immerse the entire body in water, after having proclaimed in both a loud and a low voice that this is one's intention. If one notices, after the ablution, that some part of the body remained outside the water, even though one may not know exactly which part of the body it was, the entire ritual must be repeated.

It is necessary that during ablution not one part of the body remain unwashed; however, it is not required that one wash those parts which are not visible, such as the inside of the ears or nose. In the case of ears that are pierced, the holes in them must be washed if they are large enough so the insides of them can be seen; otherwise, this is not necessary.

During ablution, one must wash the shortest hairs on the body, but it is recommended that even the longest be washed. If one washes his anus in the water of a public bath, one must first obtain the permission of the owner of this bath for the ablution to be valid. If during ablution, one breaks wind or urinates, the ritual remains valid. If one performs his ablutions after having ejaculated and one has a verse of the Qur'an or the name of Allah written or tattooed on his body, one's hand must not touch that part of the body during the ablution, but that part must be washed without being touched.

Sperm is always impure, whether it results from actual coitus or from an emission while one is either conscious or asleep, whether it is abundant or not, whether or not it results from sexual pleasure, whether emission is intentional or not.

It is recommended that one urinate after ejaculation; if one does not, the discharge that might follow one's ablution would have to be considered to be sperm, even though it seems doubtful.

During sexual intercourse, if the penis enters a woman's vagina or a man's anus, fully or only as far as the circumcision ring, both partners become impure, even if they have not reached puberty; they must consequently perform their ablutions.

If the man thinks that he has not entered the woman's vagina beyond the circumcision ring, ablution is not required.

If a man – Allah protect him from it! – fornicates with an animal and ejaculates, ablution is necessary.

If a sperm moves inside the penis but does not come out, or if there is doubt about whether it actually was emitted, ablution is not required.

A man who has ejaculated and has not yet performed his ablutions must avoid the following ten acts: eating; drinking; reading more than seven verses of the Qur'an; touching the binding of the Qur'an, or the margins of its pages, or the spaces between the lines; carrying the Qur'an on his person; sleeping; dyeing his beard with henna; anointing himself with grease or oil; having sexual intercourse after having ejaculated in his sleep.

If a man has sexual intercourse with his wife during the periods of prescribed abstinence, such as the month's fast of Ramadan, his sweat is impure, and he may not say his daily prayers while in such a state.

If a man becomes aroused by a woman other than his wife but then has intercourse with his own wife, it is preferable for him not to pray if he has sweated; but if he first has intercourse with his spouse and then with another woman, he may say his prayers even though he be in a sweat.

A man who has ejaculated as a result of intercourse with a woman other than his wife, and who then ejaculates again while having coitus with his legal wife, does not have the right to say his prayers while still sweating; but if he had intercourse with his wife first and then with a woman not his wife, he may say his prayers even though still sweating.

If a fly or any other insect settled first on something impure that is moist and then on something pure that is moist, the latter in turn becomes impure, provided one can be certain that the former was impure; failing that, it remains pure.

Besides the ablutions that are necessary and unavoidable there are a number of ablutions that are highly recommended in order to please Allah. A few of them are:

- Ablution performed Friday between dawn and noon.

- Ablution performed on the eve of the first day of Ramadan and the eves of all the odd days of that month, (third, fifth, seventh, and so on). The ablutions on the eves of the first, fifteenth, seventeenth, nineteenth, twenty-first, twenty-third, twenty-fifth, twenty-seventh, and twenty-ninth days of Ramadan are especially recommended. On the eve of the twenty-third day, one would be well advised to perform two ablutions, one at the beginning and the other at the end of the night.
- Ablution performed by a woman who has used perfume for a man other than her husband.
- Ablution of the man who has fallen asleep while in a drunken state.
- Ablution of a man or woman who, during a total eclipse of the sun or the moon, have not said their prayers.
- Ablution of one who has witnessed the hanging of a person condemned to death. If he did not witness it of his own free will, ablution is not necessarily required.

II. 15
ON THE FIVE NAMAZ

[DAILY RITUAL PRAYERS]

The person who says his five daily prayers must do so in a state of prefect concentration and complete meditation. He must abstain from committing sins such as those of jealousy, pride, or scandalmongering, or eating forbidden foods, drinking alcoholic beverages, or refusing to pay his tithes to the clergy. It is also preferable that he abstain from committing such venial sins as saying his daily prayers while half asleep or holding back his need to urinate, nor should he look up at the sky while praying. On the other hand, he would do well before praying to make sure that he has agate rings on his fingers, that he is properly dressed and well combed, that his teeth are brushed, and that he is perfumed.

While he is performing his five daily prayers, a man must make sure that, even if they cannot be seem, his genitals and his rear are covered. It is better if he covers the whole part of his body from the navel to the knees.

A woman, while saying her five daily prayers, must cover her entire body, including her head and her hair; however, it is permissible for her to leave uncovered a part of her face and hands and her feet up to the ankles.

If a man should discover, while saying his prayer, that his member is not covered, he must cover it immediately, and if that takes too much time, he must stop his prayer and start over from the beginning. But if he discovers that his member is not covered only after completing his prayer, the prayer remains valid.

During daily prayer, it is permissible to cover one's body and genitals with grass or the leaves of trees, but it is better to do this only when there are no other means at hand.

During joint prayer, the woman must position herself behind the man. If the woman and the man enter the place of worship at the same time and the woman happens to find herself in front of the man, she must say her prayer again after placing herself where she belong, i.e., behind the main.

It is highly recommended to avoid eating at the same table as one who does not attend the mosque; one must also avoid asking the advice of such a one, living near him, marrying a woman of his family, or giving him one's daughter in marriage.

It is forbidden to say one's daily prayers in the following places: a bath; saline ground; facing someone else; facing an open door; on a highway, avenue, or street; before a fireplace or lamp; in the kitchen and any other place where there is an oven; in front of a well or cesspool; facing a portrait or statue of a living model, unless these are covered; in the presence of someone who has ejaculated and has not yet performed his ablutions; in a room in which there is a photograph, even if it is not located facing the person praying; facing a grave, or on a grave, or between two graves in a cemetery.

It is not advisable to allow a feebleminded person, a child, or someone who has just eaten garlic into the mosque.

One who falls asleep while saying his prayer must say it over again if he realizes he dozed during the prayer; if he is not sure of having done so, the prayer remains valid.

Coughing, belching loudly, or sighing does not invalidate a prayer. On the other hand, the prayer is voided if one emits interjections of two letters or more.

If a person who is praying turns red in the face from suppressing an impulse to burst out laughing, that person must start the prayer over again.

If a person sobs aloud while praying because of some earthly sorrow, the prayer is invalid; but if he weeps to himself, the prayer is valid. However, if it is not over an earthly sorrow but because of the fear of Allah or the hereafter, he is urgently encouraged to weep.

Clapping one's hands or jumping up in the air during a prayer makes it null and void.

If, during prayer, one swallows bits of food left over between one's teeth, the prayer is not invalidated; but if one has a piece of sugar in his mouth and the sugar slowly melts during the prayer, the value of the latter is debatable.

During prayer, one must avoid bending one's head to the right or left, closing one's eyes, clasping one's hands, spitting, toying with one's beard, looking at the writings of the Qur'an or any other writings, or at the design of a ring. One must also avoid praying hen one feels sleepy, when one feels an urge to urinate or defecate, or when one is wearing socks that are too tight.

II. 16
On Prayers in Case of Natural Phenomenon

Namazé-ayat is the name given to the prayer to be said when one witnesses natural phenomena which inspire fear. This prayer is required in the four following cases: total or partial eclipse of the sun; total or partial eclipse of the moon; earthquake, even though it be not fearsome; thunder, lightning, and black or red winds.

If several of these phenomena occur simultaneously, for instance if an eclipse should be accompanied by an earthquake, two prayers are recovered.

In case of earthquake or lightning or thunder, one must pray immediately. Failing to do so is a sin which is not pardoned until after this prayer is said, no matter how much later, even to the last day of a person's life.

If a woman is having her period during a solar or lunar eclipse and until the eclipse is over, no prayer for this natural phenomenon is required. Nor is she obliged to say it at a later date.

II. 17
ON FASTING

Sexual intercourse is a breaking of the fast, even if the penis enters the vagina only as far as the circumcision ring, and even if no ejaculation results.

If the penis enters less deeply into the vagina and there is no ejaculation, the fast has not been broken.

If the man cannot determine with certainty what length of his penis entered into the vagina, and if he has gone in beyond the circumcision ring, his fast has not been broken.

If a man has intercourse because he has forgotten that he is in a fasting period, or if someone forces him to have intercourse, his fast has not been broken. But if he remembers the fast while the sex act is taking place, or if he is no longer forcibly constrained to complete the coitus, he must interrupt it immediately.

If a man during a fasting period masturbates and brings himself to ejaculation, his fast has been broken.

If a man ejaculates involuntarily, his fast remains valid, but if he himself does anything whatsoever to help along his involuntary ejaculation, the fast is considered to be null and void.

Taking an enema, even for medically therapeutic reasons, breaks the fast; but the use of suppositories is not forbidden; however, it is preferable to abstain from using opium suppositories.

The fast of one who, in thought, or word, or deed, bears false witness against Allah, or His Prophet or his successors, is immediately invalidated, even though he may confess on the spot to having lied and proclaim his repentance. In all likelihood, Saint Fatima [daughter of Muhammad and wife of Ali], as well as the other prophets and their successors, are also included among those against whom one may not blaspheme.

If, during the fast, one attributes in all good faith some statement to Allah or to His Prophet, and one afterward learns that his as in error, the fast remains valid. If one intentionally attributes some false quotation to Allah or to His Prophet or his successors, the fast loses its value' but if one is only repeating such a quotation heard from a third party, the fast remains valid.

The fast is invalidated if one plunges his entire head under water, but if one immerses only the right side and then the left side, the value of the fast remains intact. One's head must not be immersed in rose water; however, it may be immersed in other waters in solution, or in other liquids.

If, in order to rescue a person from drowning, one's head becomes immersed during a period of fasting, one's fast is invalidated, even if there was no other way of saving the drowning person's life.

If one has ejaculated and abstains from performing the prescribed ablutions during the vigil of the month of Ramadan, the fast loses its value.

If a person believes he ill have sufficient time, before a Ramadan vigil, to complete his ablutions after ejaculation, but discovers afterward that he does not have time enough, he may postpone his ablutions in order to begin the fast.

If a fly enters the month of a person during a period of fasting, he is not forced to take it out, if it has not gone too far into the throat; if it has remained in the mouth, he must take it out even if that causes vomiting which invalidates the fast.

If by inadvertence one eats something during the fast, and then one realizes it, one must not attempt to retrieve the part of it which has already been swallowed.

The following practices are inadvisable during fasts; putting drops in one's eyes; having a blood transfusion or taking a bath; pinching snuff or smelling aromatic plants; taking sitz baths (applies to women only); taking suppositories; getting one's clothes wet; having teeth pulled or undergoing any other surgery which might cause blood to flow into the mouth brushing one's teeth with moist wood; becoming intimate with one's wife, even without the intention of coming to ejaculation, or deliberately arousing oneself (if ejaculation is deliberately brought about, the fast is invalidated).

II. 18
On Woman and Her Periods

Woman is pseudo-menstrual hen blood is discharged from her vagina outside he time of her regular periods. The blood may be yellowish, cold, and fluid, and be discharged without any burning sensation; it may also be blackish or yellow, hot, thick, and cause a burning sensation as it passes.

Pseudo-menses are of three kinds: weak, medium, and abundant. If the blood does not fully soak a piece of cotton introduced into the vagina, the pseudo-menses are weak; if it soaks the cotton without going through to the fabric placed over the vulva, the pseudo-menses are medium; if, on the other hand , the blood soaks through both cotton and fabric, these are abundant pseudo-menses.

In the case of weak pseudo-menses, the woman must wash according to religious ritual before praying, change the cotton or ash it, and also wash her vulva if it has been soiled by the blood.

The menstrual period proper is the period of those few days during the month when blood is discharged from women's vaginas. This blood is most often thick, hot, blackish red or bright red, and gushes forth with a burning sensation.

Women of the lineage of the Prophet of Islam are menopausal at the age of sixty; others, once they are over fifty.

Blood that is discharged from the vagina of a girl under the age of nine and a woman over the age of sixty can therefore not be considered menstrual blood.

The pregnant woman and the nursing woman may have regular menstrual periods.

It is indispensable that during the first three days of the menses, the blood not be stopped from flowing; therefore, if the flow ceases after two days to resume a day later, it is not menstrual blood.

It is not indispensable that the blood flow out of the vagina for all of the three days; it is sufficient that there be some inside the vagina.

If a woman sees blood flowing from her vagina for more than three days and less than ten days, and is not sure whether this is menstrual blood or blood from an abscess, she must attempt to introduce a piece of cotton into her vagina and then withdraw it. If the blood runs out on the left side, it is menstrual blood; if on the right side, it is from the abscess.

If a woman sees blood flowing from her vagina and wonders whether it is menstrual blood or the blood of her hymen, she must introduce a piece of cotton into her vagina and leave it there for a while before withdrawing it. If the blood has spotted only the edges of the cotton, it is the blood of the hymen; if the whole piece of cotton is soaked with blood, it is menstrual.

If a woman sees blood flow from her vagina for less than three days, then stop and resume for a period of three days, then stop and resume for a period of three days, then stop and resume for a period of three days, it is this second flow which must be considered to be that of the menses, even if the first one coincided more exactly with her menstrual cycle.

During the time a woman is menstruating, it is preferable for a man to avoid coitus, even if it does not involve full penetration – that is, as far as the circumcision ring – and even if it does not involve ejaculation. It is also highly inadvisable for him to sodomize her during this time.

If the number of days of the woman's menstrual period is divided by three, a husband who has intercourse with her during the first two days must pay the equivalent of 18 *nokhods* [about 3 grams or 0.1 ounces] of gold to the poor; if he has it on the third or fourth days, the equivalent of 9 nokhods; and if he has it during the last two days, the equivalent of 4.5 nokhods.

Sodomizing a menstruating woman does not require such payment.

If a man has intercourse with his wife during all three of these periods, he must pay the equivalent in gold of 3.5 nokhods. If the price of gold has changed between the coitus and the time of payment, the rate in effect on the date of payment will prevail.

If during an act of intercourse a man notices that the woman has begun menstruating, he must withdraw; if he fails to, he must give alms to the poor.

If such a man cannot afford to give alms to the poor, he must at least give something to a beggar. If he cannot afford that either, he must ask forgiveness of Allah.

After a wife's menstrual period, her husband may repudiate her, even if she has not yet made her ablutions. He may also indulge in relations with her, but it is preferable that he wait until she has made her ablutions. In the interim, the woman is not authorized to do anything which is forbidden to her during menstruation, such as going into a mosque or touching the writing of the Qur'an, until she has completed her ablutions.

II. 19
On Marriage, Adultery, and Conjugal Relations

A woman may legally belong to a man in one of two ways; by continuing marriage or temporary marriage. In the former, the duration of the marriage need not be specified; in the latter, it must be stipulated, for example, that it is for a period of an hour, a day, a month, a year, or more.

Marriage, whether continuing or temporary, must be sealed by a religious formula spoken either by the woman or by the man, or by one of their representatives.

As long as the woman and man have not contracted a religious marriage, they are not entitled to look upon one another. To allow that, it is not enough to assume that the marriage formula has been spoken, but if the person representing them states that it has been spoken, then that is enough to validate the marriage.

If a woman authorizes someone to marry her to a man for a period of ten days, for example, without specifying the exact date, the man may contract the marriage at his pleasure, but if the woman has specified a precise day and hour, the formula must be spoken at the specified time.

The legal marriage formula must be read in Arabic, but if one cannot speak that language correctly, it may be spoken in a different language.

A father or a paternal grandfather has the right to marry off a child who is insane or who has not reached puberty by acting as its representative. The child may not annul such a marriage after reaching puberty or regaining his sanity, unless the marriage is to his manifest disadvantage.

Any girl who is of age, that is, capable of understanding what is in her own best interest, if she wishes to get married and is a virgin, must procure authorization of her father or paternal grandfather. The permission of her mother or brother is not required.

If a father or paternal grandfather marries off prepubescent son or grandson, the latter will be responsible once he has reached puberty, for taking care of his wife's material needs.

A marriage is annulled if a man finds that his wife is afflicted with one of the seven following debilities: madness, leprosy, eczema, blindness, paralysis with aftereffects, malformation of the urinary and genital tracts or of the genital tract and rectum through conjoining thereof, or vaginal malformation making coitus impossible.

If a wife finds out after marriage that her husband is suffering from mental illness, that he is a castrate, impotent, or has had his testicles excised, she may apply for annulment of her marriage.

If a wife has her marriage annulled because her husband is unable to have sexual relations with her either vaginally or anally, he must pay her as damages one-half of the dowry specified in the marriage contract. If the husband or wife annuls the marriage for any of the above-mentioned reasons, the man owes nothing to the woman if they have had sexual relations together; if they have not, he must pay her the full amount of the dowry.

It is forbidden to marry one's mother, sister, or stepmother.

It is forbidden to marry one's mother-in-law, or one's wife's maternal or paternal grandmother or any of her great-grandmothers, even though one's marriage to her may never have been consummated.

A man who marries a woman and has sexual relations with her may not marry her daughter or granddaughter, even if these be by a different marriage.

A man may not marry his wife's daughter, even if their marriage has not been consummated.

Aunts of the bride's father and the aunts of her grandparents need not wear the veil in the presence of the groom; the father, grandfather, and great-grandfather of the groom, as well as his sons, grandsons, and all his male descendants, may freely look upon the bride.

A man may not marry the nieces of his wife without the latter's consent; if he should nevertheless do so without getting consent, but his wife raises no objection, then there is no problem.

A man who has committed adultery with his aunt must not marry her daughters, that is to say, his first cousins.

If a man who has married his first cousin commits adultery with her mother, the marriage is not thereby annulled.

If a man commits adultery with a woman other than his aunt, it is highly recommended that he not marry the daughter of that woman. If he marries a woman, consummates the marriage, and then commits adultery with her mother, the marriage is not thereby annulled. Nor is it automatically annulled in the case of his having committed such adultery before the marriage was consummated, but in that case it is better if the husband voluntarily annuls the marriage.

A Muslim woman may not marry a non-Muslim man; nor may a Muslim man marry a non-Muslim woman in continuing marriage, but he may take a Jewish or Christian woman in temporary marriage.

A man who marries an already married woman must break off his marriage with her and refrain from ever marrying her again.

A married woman remains legally married after having committed adultery; however, should she not repent and should she continue to be unfaithful to her husband, it is preferable for the latter to repudiate her, but with full payment to her of her dowry.

The mother, sister, or daughter of a man who has been sodomized by another man may not marry the latter, even if both men or one of them had not yet reached puberty at the time; but if one who was the victim of the act cannot prove it, his mother, sister, or daughter is allowed to marry the other man.

If a man who has married a girl who has not reached puberty possesses her sexually before her ninth birthday, inflicting traumatisms upon her, he has no right to repeat such an act with her.

If a man sodomizes the son, brother, or father of his wife after their marriage, the marriage remains valid.

A woman who has contracted a continuing marriage does not have the right to go out of the house without her husband's permission; she must remain at his disposal for the fulfillment of any one of his desires, and may not refuse herself to him except for a religiously valid reason. If she is totally submissive to him, the husband must provide her with her food, clothing, and lodging, whether or not he has the means to do so.

A woman who refuses herself to her husband is guilty, and may not demand from him food, clothing, lodging, or any later sexual relations; however, she retains the right to be paid damages if she is repudiated.

A husband is not obligated to pay any travel expenses incurred by his wife which exceed what her expenses would have been at home; but if travel was undertaken at his own suggestion, then he must take care of the expenses.

A wife who scrupulously obeys her husband has the right to be paid the daily household expenses for any of the husband's assets, in the case the latter refuses voluntarily to pay for them. But if she is forced to meet such expenses out of her on pocket, she is not obligated to obey her husband.

A man who has contracted a continuing marriage may not leave his wife for so long a time as to allow her to question the validity if the marriage; however, he is not obligated to spend one night out of every four with her.

A husband must have sexual relations with his wife at least once in every four months.

If, at the time of contracting the marriage, no specific time was indicated at which the husband was to pay the dowry to his wife, the wife may refuse herself to her husband for so long as that amount of money has not been paid her. But once she has agreed to have sexual relations with her husband, she can no longer later refuse to, except for religiously valid reasons.

A temporary marriage, even though only one of convenience, is nevertheless legal.

A man must not abstain from having sexual relations with his temporary wife fr more than four months.

If the temporary marriage contract includes a clause specifying that the husband is not entitled to have normal sexual relations with his wife, such a clause must be respected. He must then be satisfied with giving her pleasures in other ways. But as soon as the wife consents to it, he may perform the natural sex act with her.

A woman ho has been temporarily married in exchange for a previously established dowry has no right to demand that her daily expenses be paid by her husband, even when she becomes pregnant.

A temporarily married wife may not inherit from her husband; nor may he inherit from her.

A temporarily married woman is entitled to go out of the house without asking her husband's permission, unless the fact of her so going out harms him in one way or another.

If a father (or paternal grandfather) marries off his daughter (or granddaughter) in her absence without knowing for a certainty that she is alive, the marriage becomes null and void as soon as it is established that she was dead at the time of the marriage.

It is forbidden for a man to look upon the body of a woman who is not his wife, under any pretext whatsoever. It is equally forbidden for a woman to look upon the body of a man who is not her husband.

To look upon the face and hair of a girl who has not reached puberty, if it is done without intention of enjoyment thereof, and if one is not afraid of succumbing to temptation, may be tolerated. It is however recommended that one not look upon her belly or thighs, which must remain covered.

To look upon the faces ad hands of Jewish or Christian women, if this is not done with intention of enjoyment thereof, and if one does not fear temptation, is tolerated.

A woman must hide her body and her hair from the eyes of men. It is highly recommended that she also hide them from those of prepubescent boys, if she suspects that they may look upon her with lust.

It is forbidden to look upon the genitals of another person, even from behind a glass, or in a mirror, or in standing water. It is even expressly recommended to abstain from looking at the genitals of a child who knows the difference between good and evil. But it is permitted for husband and wife to look upon each other in all parts of their bodies.

A man must not look upon the body of another man with lustful intent. Likewise, a woman may not look upon another woman with such intent.

It is not forbidden for a man to photograph a woman other than his wife, but if in order to do so he must touch her, then he must not photograph her.

If a woman is called upon to give an enema to a woman or to a man other than her husband, or to wash their genitals, then she must cover her hand so as not to come into direct contact with the genital organs; the same precautions must be taken by a man where another man or a woman other than his wife are concerned.

If a man is called upon, for medical reasons, to look upon a woman other than his wife and to touch her body, he is permitted to do so, but if he can give such care by only looking at the body he must not touch it, and if he can give it by only touching, he must not look at it.

If a man or woman be forced, in order to administer medical care, to look upon the genitals of another person, he or she must do so indirectly, in a mirror, except in case of absolute necessity.

If the husband has included in the marriage contract a clause guaranteeing his wife's virginity, he may annul the marriage if it turns out that she was not a virgin.

If a woman abjures her faith before her marriage is consummated, the marriage is annulled; the like is true after conclusion of the marriage, if she is menopausal. But if she is not menopausal and returns to her Muslim beliefs within a hundred days after the breaking off of marriage, it again becomes valid.

A man whose father or mother as a Muslim at the time of his conception, and who himself embraced the Muslim faith after reaching puberty, will have his marriage automatically abolished if he becomes an apostate.

The marriage of a man born of non-Muslim parents but who himself became a convert to Islam is automatically annulled if he renounces his faith before consummating the marriage. If he renounces his faith after having sexual relations with his wife, she must wait one hundred days after the annulment of the marriage before marrying again, if she is of age to have menstrual periods. Thus, the marriage remains valid if during those one hundred days the husband returns to the Muslim fold; otherwise, the annulment is irreversible.

If the woman inserts into the marriage contract a cause binding her husband not to mover her away from the city, and the husband accepts such a clause, then he must abide by it.

The husband of a woman who has had a daughter by a previous marriage may marry that daughter to a son of his by a previous marriage. He himself has the right to marry the mother of a girl married to his son.

A woman who becomes pregnant as a result of adultery must not have an abortion.

If a man commits adultery with an unmarried woman, and subsequently marries her, the child born of that marriage will be a bastard unless the parents can be sure it was conceived after they were married.

One need not believe a woman who claims to have entered menopause. On the one hand, she must be believed if she asserts that she is not married.

It is highly recommended that a girl be married off as soon as she reaches the age of puberty. One of the blessings of man is to have his daughter experience her first period not in her father's house, but in that of her husband.

A child born of an adulterous father is legitimate.

It is a sin to have sexual relations with one's wife during the fast of Ramadan or while she is having her menses, but the child born of such relations is legitimate.

If a man marries a woman and possesses her sexually, he may no longer marry any girl whom this woman has breast-fed.

A man may not marry a wet nurse who has breast-fed his wife.

A man may not marry a girl who was ever breast-fed by his mother or his grandmother.

The best person to breast-feed a newborn baby is its own mother. It is preferable that she not ask to be paid for such services, but that her husband pay her for it of his own free will. If the sum the mother asks for is greater than that charged by a wet nurse, the husband is free to take the child from its mother and turn it over to the wet nurse.

It is recommended that the wet nurse be a faithful Shi'ite, intelligent, modest, and pretty. On the other hand, it is most inadvisable that she be feebleminded, a nonbeliever in the Twelve Imams, ugly, or a bastard, or of bad character. It is equally inadvisable to select as wet nurse a woman who has an illegitimate child.

It is recommended that every child be breast-fed for two whole years.

II. 20
ON DIVORCE

A man who repudiates his wife must be of sound mind and past the age of puberty. He must do so of his own free will and without any constraint; thereof, if the formula for divorce is spoken in jest the marriage is not annulled.

The woman must not be having her period at the time of the divorce, and the husband must not have had sexual relations with her since her last period.

In three cases, a man may repudiate his wife while she is having her period: if he has had no sexual relations with her since their marriage; if she is pregnant while the husband believes she is having her period, and it is learned only later that she was pregnant at the time of the repudiation; if he is not certain, because of the distance that separated them, whether his wife is them having her period.

A man who has had sexual relations with his wife after her last menstrual period must wait for her to have her next one before he may divorce her. But he may divorce his wife if she has not yet reached her ninth birthday, or is pregnant, or is menopausal.

If a husband who has had sexual relations with his wife between menstrual periods, divorces her during this time and learns later that she was pregnant when the divorce took place, the latter remains valid.

A women temporarily married, say, for a month or a year, has her marriage automatically annulled at the end of that time, or at any other time when the husband releases her from the balance of her engagement. It is not necessary for this that there be any witnesses, or that the woman have had her period.

A woman who has not yet reached the age of nine or a menopausal woman may remarry immediately after divorce, without waiting the hundred days that are otherwise required.

A woman who has had her ninth birthday or who has not yet entered menopause, must wait for three menstrual periods after her divorce before being allowed to remarry.

If a woman who has not reached her ninth birthday or who has not entered menopause gets temporarily married, she must, at the end of the contract or when the husband has released her from part of it, wait two menstrual periods or forty-five days before marrying again.

If a man commits adultery with a woman he knows is not his wife, while the woman is unaware that the man is not her husband, she must wait one hundred days before remarrying.

If a man encourages a married woman to leave her husband so as to marry him, they are both committing a great sin, but the divorce and their marriage remain in force.

If the father or paternal grandfather of a boy has him marry a woman for a temporary marriage, he may prematurely cancel it in the boys interest, even if the marriage was contracted before the boy reached the age of puberty. If, for example, a fourteen-year-old boy has been married off to a woman for a period of two years, they may return her freedom to the woman before this time has run its course; but a continuing marriage cannot be broken in this way.

If a man repudiates his wife without informing her of it, and continues to meet her expenses for a period of, say, a year, and at the end of that time informs her that he got a divorce a year earlier and shows her proof of it, he may require that she return to him anything he has bought or given her during that time, provided that she has not used it up or consumed it, in which case he cannot demand its return.

II. 21
On the Mortuary Ritual

If a part of the body becomes detached, whether after or before death, and one touches such a part when the cleansing of the corpse has not yet been completed, one must undergo a purifying ablution; but this is not necessary if the part of the body involved is boneless.

If one touches a bone or a tooth removed from a corpse, ablution is necessary; but it is not required if the bone or tooth was removed from a live body, unless there is a muscle attached to it.

One must avoid leaving a dying person alone, placing a heavy object on his belly, leaving him in the care of a man who has ejaculated or a woman who is having her period, speaking too much in his presence, weeping, or leaving him in the sole care of women.

Ablution of a dead man by a woman, or visa versa, is forbidden. But the woman may perform this ritual if the man is her husband, and the man in the case of his own wife. However, it is preferable that they do not do it.

It is forbidden to look upon the sexual organs of a dead man or woman. The person performing the ablution ritual commits a cardinal sin if he violates this ban, but the ablution does not thereby lose its validity.

During the ritual, the genitals of the corpse must remain covered, even if only by a piece of wood or a brick.

If a person dies in a well and it is impossible to get the body out, the well must be shut off and become his tomb.

If a child dies within the mother's womb and it is a danger to her life to leave it there, it must be extracted in the easiest way possible; it can, if need be, be cut into pieces; this should be done either by the woman's husband or by a woman of this profession.

One has no right to exhume the body of a Muslim, not even that of a child or of a madman, unless it has turned to dust.

One may exhume a body if it is done in order to remove a still living child from its mother's womb, or if there is danger that a wild animal may devour it, or that a flood may carry it away, or that it may fall into the hands of the enemy. One may also reopen a sepulcher in order to deposit in it a part of the departed one's body which has been found or recovered after burial.

II. 22
On Finance and Taxes

All commercial transactions which involve any of the following are declared null and void: trade in urine, excrement, or alcoholic beverages; trade in misappropriated wealth, unless the owner thereof agrees to it; trade in anything other than merchandise; trade in musical instruments or gambling accessories; trade based upon interest produced by a sum of money; sale of any adulterated merchandise, unless the buyer is informed of the fact in advance.

Trade in oil, curative solutions, and perfumes imported from non-Muslim countries is allowed, provided that their impurity has not been proven; on the other hand, fat is impure if it is produced in an Islamic country and comes form an animal which has not been established to have been slaughtered according to Muslim ritual. Trade in such products is illegal.

There can be no trade in skins of foxes which died or were slaughtered in manners contrary to Muslim ritual.

Trade in meat, fat, and skins is allowed, provided the seller is a Muslim; but it is forbidden if the buyer knows that this Muslim got them from an infidel, unless it is formally established that the animals were killed in accordance with the rules prevailing in Islam.

Any trade in objects for enjoyment, such as musical instruments, however small they may be, is strictly illegal.

A Muslim is allowed to require payment by an infidel of interest on money that he has lent him. This is also allowed between father and child, and between husband and wife.

Persons who work oil deposits, or gold, silver, lead, copper, iron, turquoise, salt or other mines must pay the *khoms* [one-fifth tax on income] to the Islamic Treasury provided the income therefrom reaches the required minimum. This minimum must be the equivalent in value of coins comprising 415 grams of silver or 45 grams of gold, after deduction of expenses. If the income does not reach such a figure, the *khoms* is still due if the gross income exceeds annual expenses.

Anyone who discovers treasure the value of which is at least that of coins of 415 grams of silver or 45 grams of gold must also pay the *khoms* to the Islamic Treasury.

If a person buys an animal and thereafter discovers in its belly some valuable object, he must first inquire of the seller whether that objects belongs to him. If it does not, he must check back with previous owners. If it turns out that the object belongs to none of them, he must pay the khoms, even if the price of the object is less than 415 grams of silver or 45 grams of gold.

If someone dives into a river, such as the Tigris or Euphrates, and comes up with a jewel, he must pay the *khoms* on its value, provided that such rivers are known customarily to contain such jewels.

If a person dives and comes up with a quantity of amber of value in excess of 4 grams of gold, he must pay the *khoms* on it, even if it was the result of more than a single dive.

If a child discovers a mine or a treasure or finds a jewel under water, his father or guardian must pay the *khoms* on it.

The income from the *khoms* collected throughout the country is to be divided between *Seyed* [descendants of the Prophet] and the Holy Imam, represented in our time by a *Modjtahed* [learned man]. The *Seyed*'s share is to be meted out, with the *Modjtahed*'s permission, to poor *Seyed*, orphaned *Seyed*, and ruined *Seyed*. The Imam's share may be spent only with the permission of his representative on earth, the *Modjtahed*.

The *zakat* [obligatory alms – tax] for camels is to be computed on the basis of twelve brackets:

1) one sheep for five camels;
2) two sheep for ten camels;
3) three sheep for fifteen camels;
4) four sheep for twenty camels;
5) five sheep for twenty-five camels;
6) one second-year camel for twenty-six camels;
7) one third-year camel for thirty-six camels;
8) one fourth-year camel for forty-six camels;
9) one fifth-year camel for sixty-one camels;
10) two third-year camels for seventy-six camels;
11) two fourth-year camels for ninety-nine camels;
12) for 120 camels or more, one must figure one three-year-old camel for every forty camels, or one four-year-old camel for every fifty camels, or calculate by brackets for fifty and forty, being very careful not to overlook any, and, if there are any left over, that the remainder be no more than nine. For example, if one owns 140 camels, he must give two four-year-old camels, for the first hundred and one three-year-old camel for the remaining forty. All camels given in payment of the *zakat* must be females.

II. 23
ADDENDUM

Shaving one's face, whether bladed razors or electric apparatuses intended for the same purpose, is highly unacceptable.

Beating of drums during athletic contests is not allowed; nor is the playing of military music during military ceremonies, if such music can in any way be assimilated to licentious music.

Gambling is forbidden, even if indulged in not for gain but merely as an amusement.

No Muslim is permitted to work in a Jewish concern, if he knows, or has the slightest suspicion, that this concern gives support to Israel. Money thus earned is impure.

It is not strictly forbidden for Muslims to work for a concern managed by a Muslim which also employs Jews, provided the worker does not serve Israel in any manner whatsoever. However, it is shameful to do one's work under the orders of a Jewish foreman.

It is absolutely forbidden to dissect the corpse of a Muslim, but the dissection of non-Muslim corpses is acceptable.

The flesh of any animal slaughtered by the methods in various countries, where recently available machines are employed, is impure, and it is forbidden to either sell or to buy it. In such a transaction, the seller owes the buyer the money he paid for it, even if the animal was slaughtered while facing in the direction of Mecca, and even if the name of Allah was invoked at the time.

Any meat imported from the countries of the infidels is strictly impure, and considered the same as the flesh of a corpse, unless it is proven that the cattle was slaughtered according to Muslim ritual.

It is forbidden to look upon a woman other than one's wife, or an animal, or a statue, in a sensual or lubricious manner.

A woman who wishes to pursue her studies toward the end of being able to earn her living though respectable work, and who has a male teacher, may do so if she keeps her face covered and has no contact with men; but if that is inevitable, and religious and moral tenets are thus undermined, she must give up her studies.

Girls and boys who attend coeducational classes in grammar schools, high schools, universities, or other teaching establishments, and who, in order to legalize such a situation, wish to contract a temporary marriage may do so without the permission of their fathers. The same applies if the boy and girl are in love but hesitate to ask for such permission.

Printed in Dunstable, United Kingdom

71846094R00045